July's Thick Kingdom

⁂

Kathleen Brewin Lewis

FUTURECYCLE PRESS

www.futurecycle.org

Published by FutureCycle Press
Lexington, Kentucky, USA

ISBN 978-1-942371-10-6

For Jeff, a man for all seasons.

Contents

Truly the light is sweet,
and a pleasant thing it is for the eyes to behold the sun.

—*Ecclesiastes 11:7*

Narrow Escape

Languor of lingerie, parsing of pearls,
whistle and whir of the wind.
A tapering of the long road before you,
crush of the sky round the bend.

Forsake threadbare paths, the furrows
of protocol, sorrow of window and pane.
Encircle the season you seek to dismantle,
the lair of your life in the rain.

Grit of the pear on the tip of your tongue,
scintilla of smoke in your hair.
Sensation of strength, premonition of mercy,
a descant of steps on the stair.

Pawn your blue velvet cloak.
Disappear into the trees.

January's hair

is gray and thin, frizzes over the river,
tangles in the bare trees.
She places a hex over the land,
cloaks it in slush and ice, renders
it colorless. Her bitter breath
withers the grass, stiffens
the birds on their roosts. And yet,
I owe her. She keeps me inside
a calescent tower, frequently gifts me
a slim slant of sunlight, heightens
my senses by banishing the frivolous,
calls me to let down my hair.

Inside the Polar Vortex, Atlanta

> *Thus he gives snow like wool,*
> *scatters hoarfrost like ashes,*
> *sends crystals of ice like crumbs of bread —*
> *who can withstand such cold?*
> *—from Psalm 147, Complete Jewish Bible*

Black ice, swirling wind. Tree limbs crack,
    down the power lines. We are cold
        and full of questions—how to drive,
            where are our gloves, who's to blame?

We fishtail, stall
    on tractionless roads,
        long for home—
            until we get there.

The logs in the fireplace
    burn down to ash. We read
        by candlelight or not at all,
            sup on boredom served
                at brisk room temperature. Still

a soft white blanket coats
    the lawn and roof, and there's
        a crimson scarf on the snowman,
            bread crumbs to be scattered
                for the huddled, muted birds.

Still

I'm still waiting for you to appear in the feathery clouds,
my heaven-gone father.

I'm still waiting for you to appear in the feathery clouds,
my heaven-gone father.
—Cecilia Woloch

Spring arrives early where we come from,
on the fat-oaked, moss-draped coast.
At your burial in late February, the azaleas
were already blooming, sand gnats circling
in the warm Geechee air. I was hot
with grief and anger; your winter
had come too soon.

In the eighteen years since, you have sent:
one spectacular rainbow arching over the marsh,
a soft and unexpected snowfall, a lone heron
watching from a drought-drained pond.
I don't expect signs any more, still
send up prayers, ask you to guide
my children as they make their way
through this obstacled world.

If you are reading this over my shoulder—
and I like to think you are—I want to tell you
that spring has come early again this year.
Bulbs have burst through the ground
to scent this place; palmettos clatter
in the breeze. Though I have learned
to bury anger, in this warmed soil
my grief blooms still.

Make Believe

Once I believed in emblems. Signs and portents. The sound of the owl the night you left. A shard of blue eggshell on the path. The blood moon after I miscarried. Now I only believe in coincidence. If *believe* is even the right word. The spare change you deposit on your dresser each evening? What if it were the vexing events of the day, the misspoken words you no longer had use for? Pinfeathers in the hand; two birds in the bush. Empty your pockets. Look, here's a nickel minted the very year you were born.

Interior Scene with Family & Small Bird

Once when you and your brother were small,
we filled a plastic feeder with sweet red water.
I climbed the stepladder, hung it
outside the dining room window.

You weren't sure you'd seen a hummingbird before,
so your brother described one to you:
How tiny it was, how quick. How its wings
beat so fast, they disappeared.

We were vigilant at mealtimes, looked up at every bite.
Then one supper, after we'd said grace and you were
telling your dad about your day—the books you'd brought home
from the preschool library, the classroom hedgehog—
one appeared, fairy-like, treading air beside the feeder.

You sucked in your breath;
the four of us exchanged sideways glances.
Everybody freeze, I whispered,
laying one finger across my lips.
But of course, we didn't.

56th Spring

The day is florid beyond all recalling. Daffodils
have given way to clouds of dogwoods,
but forsythia still blazes, and azaleas—
cerise, salmon, rosy dawn—are saying *ah*
and showing their throats.

Wisteria hangs languid and lavender
among the sweetgums and yellow pollen
dusts the ivy's bottle green, piles,
puddles on the sidewalk.

I see I've left pale footprints
on the floor of my empty house,
tracked part of this fecundity indoors.
I turn slowly and stare hard at the trace marks,
thinking them mockery, some kind of joke.

The Penitent at Fourteen

In the tender summer darkness
she kneels on sharp grass.
Her fingertips are her rosary beads.

The rise and fall of cricket song
prickles the skin on her arms. She hopes
her quarrelling parents will not notice
her absence as she drops to her knees
beyond the cast of houselight.

Honeysuckle soaks the air, obscene to her,
cloying. Mosquitoes hum at her neck,
their bites her stigmata.

She prays for the legions of poor and lonely,
an injured classmate, her cancerous uncle.
For an antidote to the rift in her home.
She begs to be granted absolution.

And what is her sin exactly,
this chaste girl with scant breasts?
Not sloth, nor wrath, nor gluttony.
No dishonor or false witness borne.
Just this: that she presumes to carry
the weight of the world on her slight shoulders.

The pulsing white stars spread across the sky.
She wishes one of them would fall
so she could pray for it, too.

Luna Moth

She has one week to live.

The first night, she appears
at my window: finch-sized,
owl-spotted, swallow-tailed.
Astounding me with her
vivid green beauty.

Mouthless, she is not driven
by ordinary hunger. She craves
moonlight and streetlight, mates
after midnight, leaves legions
of eggs on the underside of
black walnut leaves.

Her caterpillar offspring
will never know her.
After the seventh day, I find her
in the grass, lime wings
faded to celadon and tattering
in the wind.

In June, summer

circles back like a canyon condor.
The precocious valley greens
with Queen Anne's lace and clover,
droning bees, clicking grasshoppers.

Late-blooming mountains are still
dark with conifers, their highest ground
pale with morning frost. The fox's kits
huddle in their hillside den. Before long

they will make their way down
to the sundrenched valley, leap
through tall grass, feast on lizards,
dewlaps flashing bright as berries.

July's Thick Kingdom

Chalice of cherries,
bloody juice on the chin.
A sorcerer's crumbling of mint.
The brown hare spent
and snagged in the bramble,
the huntsman's lost arrow bent.
Crown of clouds, throne of honeysuckle,
flask of dandelion wine. The falcon
alights on a gauntlet of broom moss.
Sunset flares through the regal pines.

In the dwindling glow, fireflies.
In the raptor's beak, a golden coin.

Auguries of August

The river has slipped over its banks
and into the woods.
Its quiet darkness laps the shins
of the old-growth pines.
The oak whispers to the spotted owl:
*Better build your nest as high
as possible.* The spotted owl
murmurs to the oak: *If fish come,
it will have begun to be over.*

And what of the field mice?

The water ripples.
The breeze holds its breath.
The river has slipped over its banks
and into the woods.

And so, September

arrives to straddle the seasons—
parching heat, then spattering rain,
too late to save the corn but in time
to sprout the pumpkin. There will be
plenty of down-to-earth suns to sell
at fall farmers markets, hickory nuts
and collards, cured hams and radishes,
amber jars of honey. Dahlias wrapped
in dampened newsprint; cinnamon-laced pies.
The solstice has been recalled, the equinox
advances. Soon—a heady whiff
of wood smoke. Yellow leaves stunning
the black pond.

Petrichor

Two geologists made this word
from the Greek: *petros,* for stone,
and *ichor,* for the liquid that flows
through the veins of the gods.
They wanted to name the scent
of parched earth after fresh rain:
the reconstituted redolence
of salted silt marbled
with terracotta; this old,
dry world brought
back to loamy life.
Another name for mercy.

Firefall

Off and on from 1872 to 1968, at 9:00 p.m. sharp,
visitors to Yosemite National Park were treated
to a cascade of fire from Glacier Point.

Before they finally burned down to embers,
she wished someone had pushed them
off a 3,000-foot cliff at night
like the lodge workers used to do
with the summer bonfires
at Yosemite. Make a glowing,
pulsing cataract of them—red sparks
streaming through dark sky,
a brief brilliant marvel.

Better than their slow descent
into a scant gray pile
of cinders.

Rite of Passage on Red Top Mountain

Somewhere along the trail my son has passed me, and now I follow
him. His muscling calves disappear around a bend. A few minutes
later he calls to me—*Mama? Coming,* I say. He waits until I'm in
sight to turn back to the path. Half a mile more, all birdsong ceases.
There's a man just inside the woods, a sullen stag dressed in a
sleeveless T-shirt and dirty jeans, arms covered in crude tattoos.
He stares at me but does not speak. Heart races; legs will not. I glimpse
my son, standing a few yards up the path. *Come on, Mom,* he says
in a doughty voice. When I catch up to him, he puts one arm around
my waist, shows me the pocket knife in his other hand. We don't
look back.

Shoulder Season

Autumn rode into town on a chestnut mare,
an aubergine crow on his shoulder.
I saw him coming through a field of goldenrod,
cricket chorus screeching hosannas.
Hey, I waved. *Hey, Autumn!*
I'm so glad you're here—it's been so hot.
He looked me over, asked if I wanted a ride,
pulled me up across the horse's rump.
The crow lifted, circled overhead.

I put my arms around his waist. He smelled like hay
and cold creeks. *I'm not necessarily here to stay,*
he allowed, *just scouting things out,*
putting the squirrels on notice. He pointed
at some sumac, which reddened.
Then he asked for a kiss. Turned around
in the saddle while I leaned forward.
His lips were dry as old leaves. *Hell, you taste*
like one of them little spring trout lilies,
he muttered. *I better let you off here.*

I swung my leg over and slid off the horse.
See you later, then, I said, *but don't stay gone too long.*
Oh, I won't, Missy. You'll see. I'll be back
before you know it. He snapped his fingers.
The crow settled back on his shoulder;
the mare moved forward. They ambled
up a rise into the woods.

Sisyphus in Autumn

Dry leaves layer the lawn,
scuttle in the wind,
like crabs across the concrete.
The rain decoupages them
into slick patterns on the driveway.

Because he treasures his acre of suburbia,
he labors for hours to uncover
the smooth carpet of dim grass,
clear the ragged piles from the sidewalk.
It looks really nice now, I tell him, as he hangs
the blower on a hook in the carport, removes
the protective earphones from his head.
But even as I say this, I can see over his shoulder—
a few leaves stealing back onto our property,
as if the trees were coyly dropping crisp handkerchiefs.

In a few days, he will begin again.

The Old Beach House

We rented my family's old beach house last October, the one my
father sold fifteen years ago when we learned his cancer had spread.
The white clapboard house was nicer than it used to be, with a new
bathroom and a better kitchen, but the dark paneled walls were still
warm and rich; the front windows framed the same Back River sunset.
I could swear I saw my little girl climb out of the bathtub and toddle
into the bedroom, her head ringed in wet curls, baby bottom bare
and round, fat little feet slapping the wood floor. But when I followed
her into the room, there was just a young woman standing there in
jeans and a soft sweater, brushing her long blonde hair in front of
the mirror.

Downing the Sun

In the west now, a searing sunset
illumines the imprint of your breast on mine.
There have you traveled on purpose without me,
no forwarding address, no departing line.
Is this the glimmer for which you betrayed me?
Can you remember the slant of our sky?
Walking as straight as your tall boots will let you,
shed shards of moonrise, a husked lullaby.
I have been cauterized, left in the shadows,
longing for glimpses of walnuts and gorse.
If I sing softly, will dragonflies nestle me,
grant me sweet amnesty from this remorse?

I don a crown of mountaintops, leap heavily
into the evening sea, still do not drown.

A Brace of Weeping Women

—A sod widow has lost her husband due to his death; a grass widow has been abandoned.

I. The Sod Widow Revises Her Vows

This rind of moon
casts little light,
a darkness still
less than yours.

I will not think
of your flensed limbs,
your soft eyes
turned to quartz.

If I could dream,
I'd flesh you out,
relish the weight of you,
the warmth.

It has rained for days,
seeped deeply down
into sated ground.
I have pledged

to tend you always,
scythe the grass
that creeps
to conceal your grave.

II. The Grass Widow Grows Weary

How I wish
this gravid moon
would burst
and offer me relief.

I grieve to picture
your body on hers,
recall the rawness
of our youth.

If I could forget,
I would remember
to sleep, remember
to swallow my food.

I grow green
with bitterness,
lurch barefoot
across hapless earth,

water my pasture
with tears. I dig
a profound hole,
bury hope, stone love.

Old Wife's Tale

She could usually tell which women still had them by the trimness
of their waists, the glow of their skin. It was commonly called
The Curse, the monthly flow of warm thick fluids, the crimson
smear that proved you were vital and potent, bloody but unbowed.
They should call it The Blessing, she thought. When it's your time of
the month, it means you're having the time of your life. Smooth throat,
full breasts, a way of walking in the world as if your womb were full
of possibility. Sometimes she just wanted to slap those young wives
in the face.

The Poet at Fifty-Nine

—after Larry Levis

Autumn is a glum raisin,
plumped with sweet wine,
stirred into a spiced batter.
As the cake bakes, scents rising,
I think of the woman
who taught me to make it,
of everything I learned
from all the old women:
how to seed zinnias and play canasta,
make artichoke relish and ambrosia,
tie French knots, polish the silver;
the hemming and pressing of skirts.

These women spun stories
on the porch in evening,
waiting for the house to cool.
Hung strips of foil on grapevines
so bluejays wouldn't steal the ripe fruit.
Snatched clothes off lines before storms struck,
wrote letters to men at war. They learned to swim
through disappointment in green creeks,
and some spoke, softly, of babies they'd lost.

The first dark has entered the trees,
diminishing their saffron glow.
I've mixed a cocktail, opened a can of almonds
to eat with the warm cake. My thoughts meld
with the murmurings of the old women,
in the dim parlors of memory.

The words go on, a braided rope.
Lessons have been learned.
The grapevines are bare.
The land is mine.

Bones to Pick

The old couple picks at the day
as if it were a roasted chicken.
They dine on the breast at breakfast,
devour the liver, heart, and gizzard at lunch,
are down to the dark meat for dinner.
Then the real nibbling and gnawing begins.
They pull the last shreds of meat from the ribs,
pry the morsels from the wings. One of them
wrests the wishbone from the greasy carcass
and holds it aloft. She wants to paint it gold
and hang it on a ribbon, but he calls for the question,
there and then. *What's your wish?* he demands,
Pick a side and pull. And so, with a crack of the cartilage,
it is decided: which one will turn in for the evening,
which one will sit alone in the dark.

Nocturne

My mother used to walk as if to music, as if she knew someone were watching. They always were. Tonight she cannot sleep. She goes into her study, shuffles through papers, pens her signature. In the morning, she will show me she has put her life in my hands. She will give me the key to the safe deposit box, tell me she hides her finest jewelry in a quilted pink case under the sofa, hand me a list of her favorite hymns. And I will touch her face, which is still beautiful.

The crook of your arm

is warm and surely you are
thick bread, sweet butter
the sun at noon
brown hawk in the sky
the Cliffs of Dover
oak logs, split and stacked
oversized sweater with
leather patches
scent of copper
salt water
cairn marking the trail
solitary lighthouse
its beam
Thanksgiving dinner
rain in the night.

Illumination on I-285

Beside the curving exit ramp
that links one interstate to the next,
an enclave of office buildings
rises up in the cold dark:
a great grid of white lights
blazing in the night.
Perhaps because it's Christmas—
car radio casting carols—
the shining island seems
a holy city and I hear
pure shaped notes
coming through the airwaves—
Gloria, Gloria, in excelsis Deo—
receive the gift
of the traveling moment,
where all is calm and
all is bright.

Acknowledgments

My thanks to the following journals and their editors for publishing my poems, some in slightly different versions:

Appalachian Heritage: "Luna Moth," "The Poet at Fifty-Nine"

Boston Literary Review: "Old Beach House" (formerly "Haunted House"), "Old Wife's Tale"

Broad River Review: "A Brace of Weeping Women" (Finalist, 2014 Ron Rash Poetry Award)

Cider Press Review: "Downing the Sun"

Curio Poetry: "Sisyphus in Autumn"

Loose Change Magazine: "Bones to Pick"

Menacing Hedge: "Make Believe," "Narrow Escape," "Firefall"

The Christian Century: "Petrichor"

The Southern Women's Review: "Interior Scene with Family and Small Bird"

Still: The Journal: "In June, summer," "July's Thick Kingdom," "Auguries of August," "And so, September"

Verse-Virtual: "Nocturne," "Rite of Passage on Red Top Mountain," "The crook of your arm"

I'm always grateful to and for my supportive family—Jeff, Ben, Rosalee, and my mother, Norma. Wright's Writers and the Side Door Poets have offered helpful ideas on individual poems in workshops. *Still* Poetry Editor Marianne Worthington has been generous with opportunities. And my friend and teacher, the poet William Wright, continues to prompt, inspire and encourage me. Thank you all.

Cover design by Rosalee Lewis; author photo by Keiko Guest Photography; interior book design by Diane Kistner; Caudex text and titling

About FutureCycle Press

FutureCycle Press is dedicated to publishing lasting English-language poetry books, chapbooks, and anthologies in both print-on-demand and ebook formats. Founded in 2007 by long-time independent editor/publishers and partners Diane Kistner and Robert S. King, the press incorporated as a nonprofit in 2012. A number of our editors are distinguished poets and writers in their own right, and we have been actively involved in the small press movement going back to the early seventies.

The FutureCycle Poetry Book Prize and honorarium is awarded annually for the best full-length volume of poetry we publish in a calendar year. Introduced in 2013, our Good Works projects are anthologies devoted to issues of universal significance, with all proceeds donated to a related worthy cause. Our Selected Poems series highlights contemporary poets with a substantial body of work to their credit; with this series we strive to resurrect work that has had limited distribution and is now out of print.

We are dedicated to giving all of the authors we publish the care their work deserves, making our catalog of titles the most diverse and distinguished it can be, and paying forward any earnings to fund more great books.

We've learned a few things about independent publishing over the years. We've also evolved a unique, resilient publishing model that allows us to focus mainly on vetting and preserving for posterity the most books of exceptional quality without becoming overwhelmed with bookkeeping and mailing, fundraising activities, or taxing editorial and production "bubbles." To find out more about what we are doing, come see us at www.futurecycle.org.

www.ingramcontent.com/pod-product-compliance
Lightning Source LLC
Chambersburg PA
CBHW060044050426
42448CB00012B/3118